FOOD AND FARMING

A chronological study from the Romans to modern times

Richard Dawson

A Piccolo Original
Piccolo Books

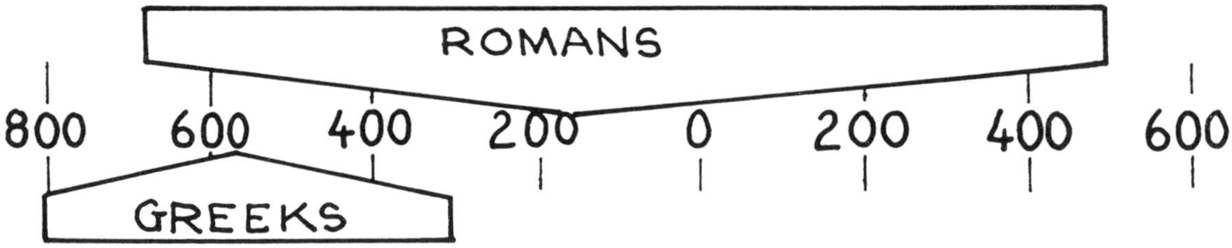

THE GREEKS

The Greek diet was simple; only small amounts of meat were eaten by common people as it was very expensive. Meat was mainly imported from Italy although sometimes, after a sacrifice, the meat would be butchered and distributed to the poor. Barley was the only grain crop that was home grown; it was used to make porridge and barley bread. Wheat was imported from Italy and the bread it made was very expensive and eaten only by the rich people. Fish were caught locally and eaten by most people. A lot of fruit, e.g. pomegranates, dates, figs, grapes, olives, apples; and vegetables e.g. beans, chick-peas, turnips, leeks and salad were grown and eaten.

Most of the cooking was done outside in the courtyard either by the women or the household slaves. Food was either fried in olive oil or stewed over an open fire. The shopping, however, was done by the men in the *agora* – which was the main market area in the town. The rich had splendid feasts – but only for the men! Food was served by slaves and the only ladies present were the ones who provided the entertainment.

Greece is a land of mountains and small plains. On the rocky ground surrounding the plains the farmers had herds of goats and flocks of tough mountain sheep, which were reared for skins and meat. Greek farmers had a hard life; they worked the rich soil of the plains with their ploughs, which were pulled by oxen.

The wealth of a farmer was often judged by the number of oxen he owned. His other valuable assets were his olive trees and grape vines, which grew well on the red soils. The farmers lived in fear of drought

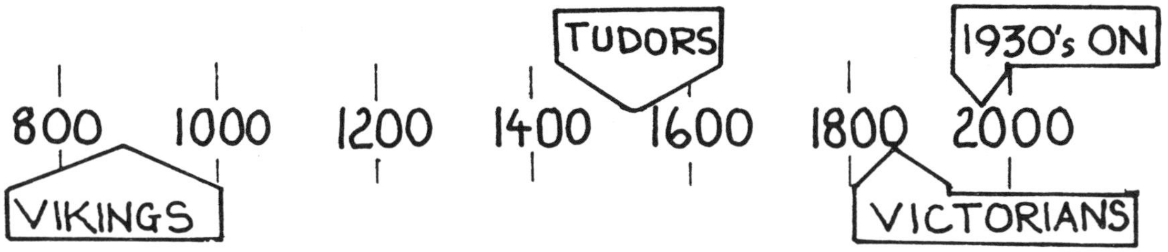

and crop failure – it was then they had to sell their land and work on it for the rich land owners. By the eighth century BC most of Greece was owned by the rich and worked by peasant farmers.

You are invited to the feast, make your way there collecting all the food on the way. You can only go through each door once!

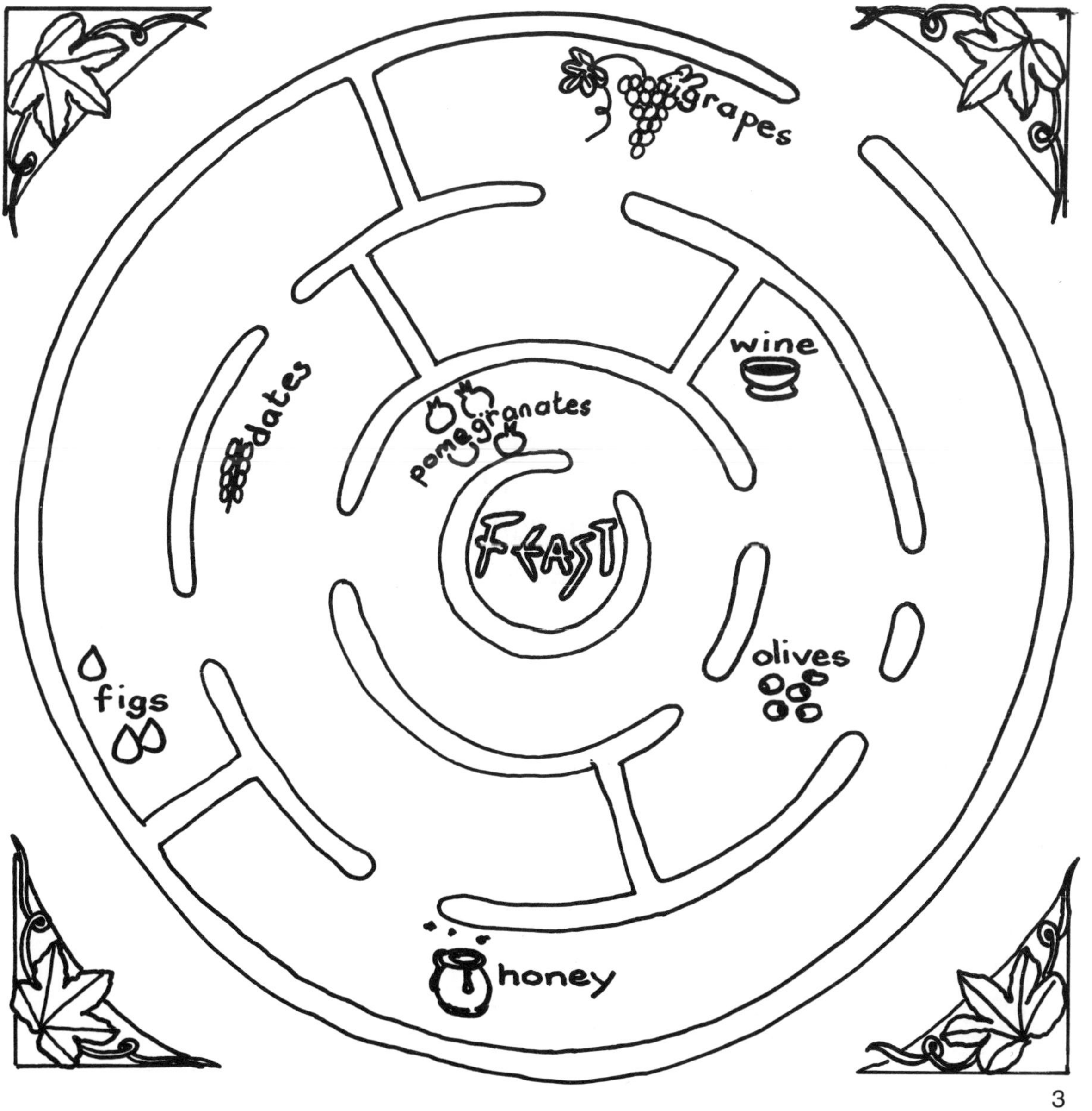

ACROPOLIS RESTAURANT

When did the Greek people eat these?
Breakfast, lunch or dinner?

Home or Away?

If you think that the Greeks produced the food, join it to the plough . . . if it was imported, join it to the ship.

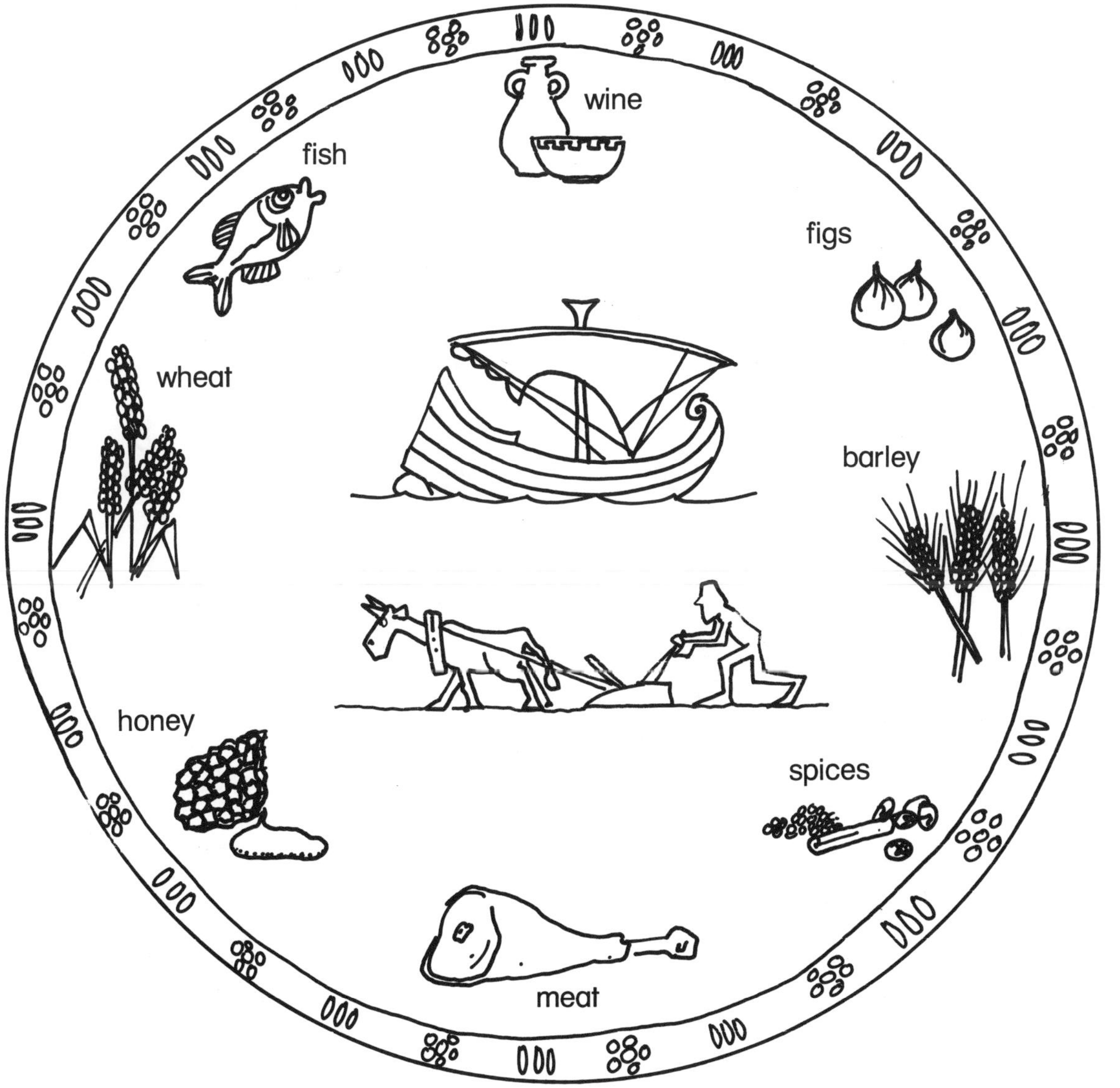

Which of these animals were found on Greek farms?

Yes/No

Yes/No

Yes/No

Yes/No

Yes/No

Some Greek Crops . . .

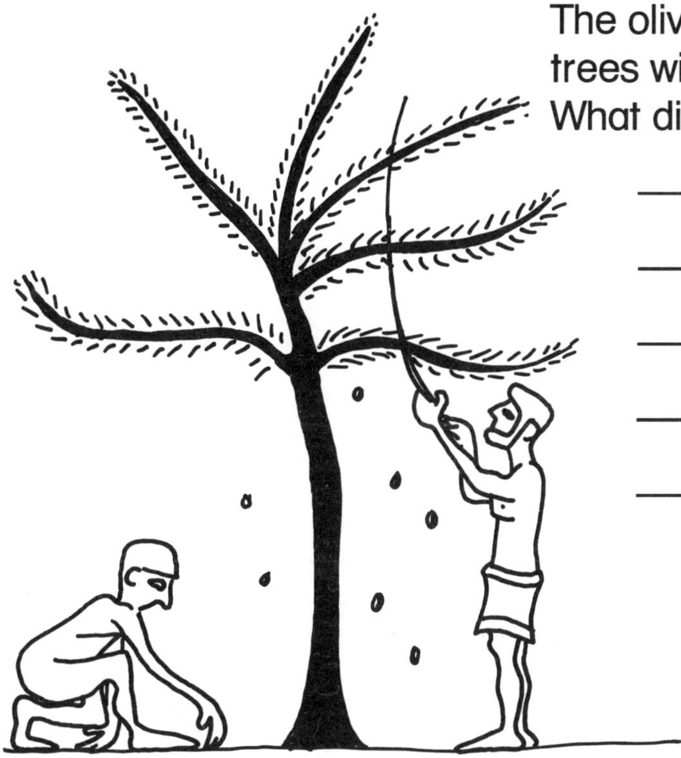

Olive Harvest

The olives were knocked from the trees with long sticks.
What did the Greeks use olives for?

____

____

____

____

____

Grapes

Grapes grow on vines and need lots of sunshine to make them ripen.
What did the Greeks use grapes for?

____

____

____

____

____

THE ROMANS

A Roman called Martial planned a meal for seven of his friends. He decided to have lettuce, leeks, mint, chicory, parsley, beans and marrows. To accompany this he planned to prepare milk-fed snails, suckling pig, lamb meat balls, ham, chicken, boiled goose and dormouse – a special Roman delicacy!

The Romans grew all their own vegetables and fruit in their very organized gardens. Here is Martial's garden . . . plant it for him!

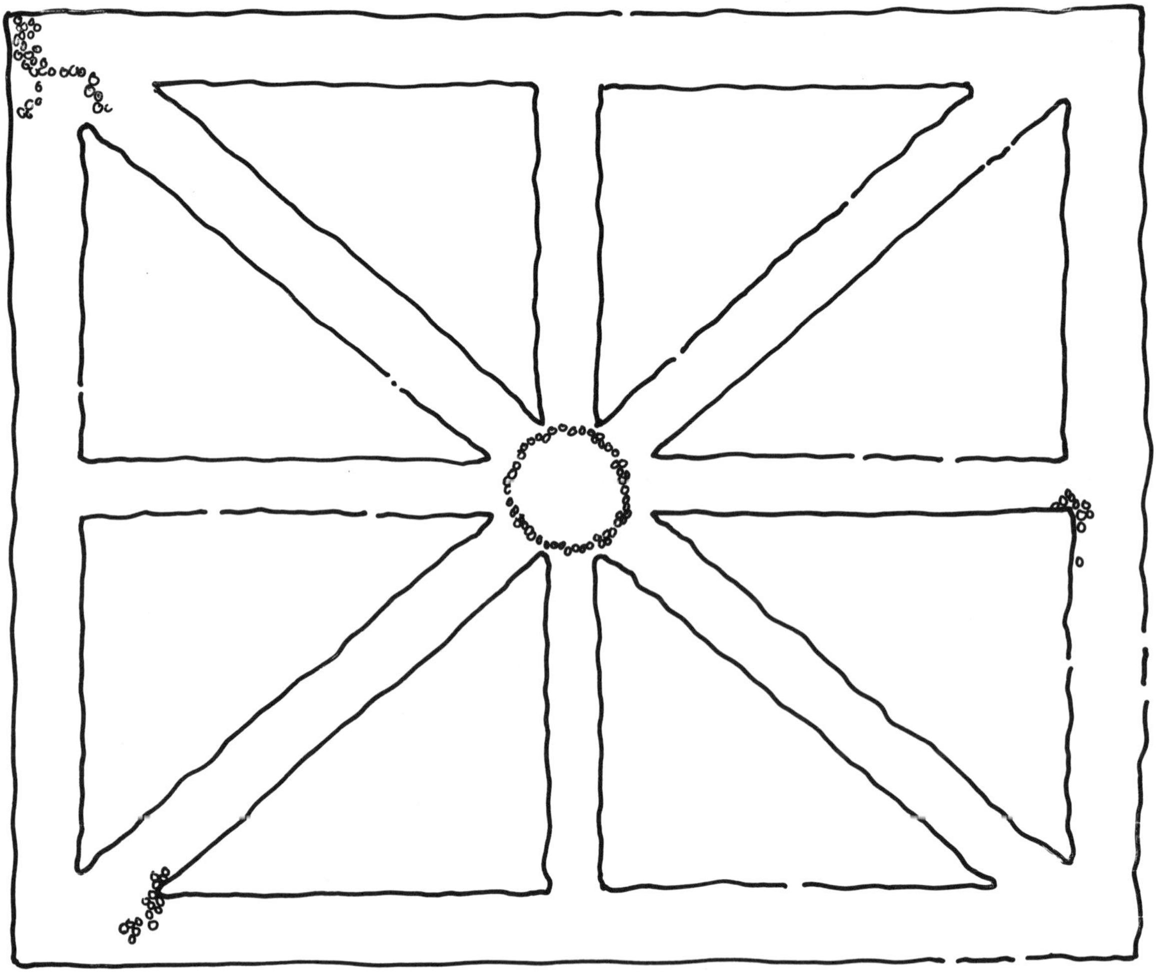

All the meat came from Martial's own farm.
Draw the farm animals here!

What do you think Martial looked like?

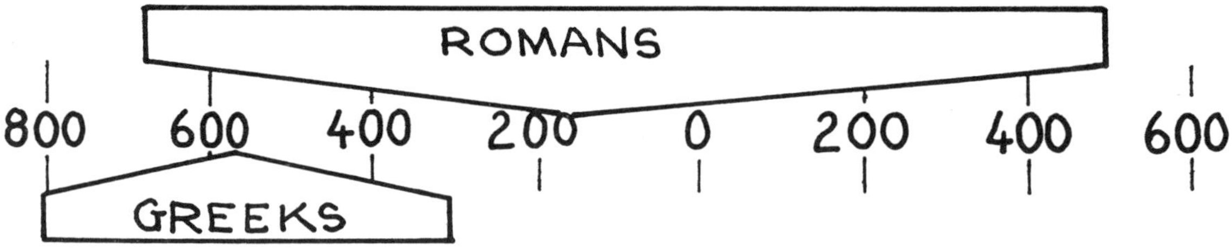

THE VIKINGS

Viking farmers were completely self-sufficient. They made all their own clothes from linen or from wool from their own sheep. They raised all their own animals and caught their own fish. They grew their own crops – rye, oats, barley, wheat, peas, beans and cabbage and collected wild leeks and garlic.

Vikings only ate two meals a day. When do you think they ate?

Vikings ate huge quantities of meat and drank vast quantities of mead – a wine made from honey – the drinking horns could not be put down until they were empty!

The Vikings used a lot of salt in their meals. Where do you think they got it from?

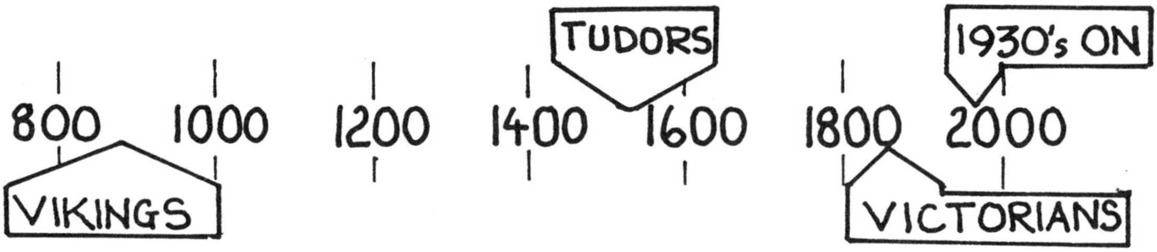

In Viking times farmers' fields were divided into strips – each strip was planted with a different crop.
Plant your fields . . .

What about the next year? Do you think they planted the same crops in the same strip? ____________________

All these things were dug up at Jorvik – the Viking settlement now called York.

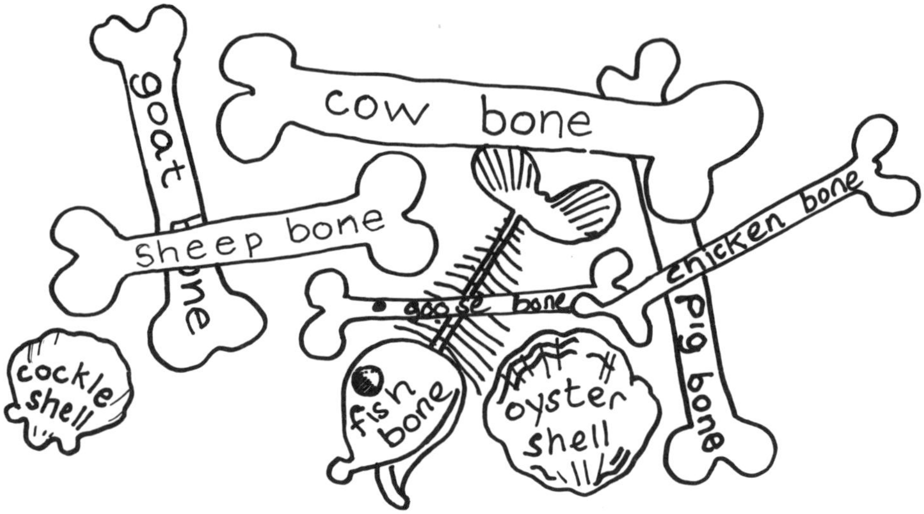

What do they tell you about Viking meals?

___

___

___

The archaeologists also found the remains of oats, barley, wheat, rye, apples, plums, blackberries, hazelnuts, carrots, celery, beans and peas!

These remains were found somewhere rather unpleasant – can you guess where?

___

___

___

Draw six animals which you think lived on Viking farms.

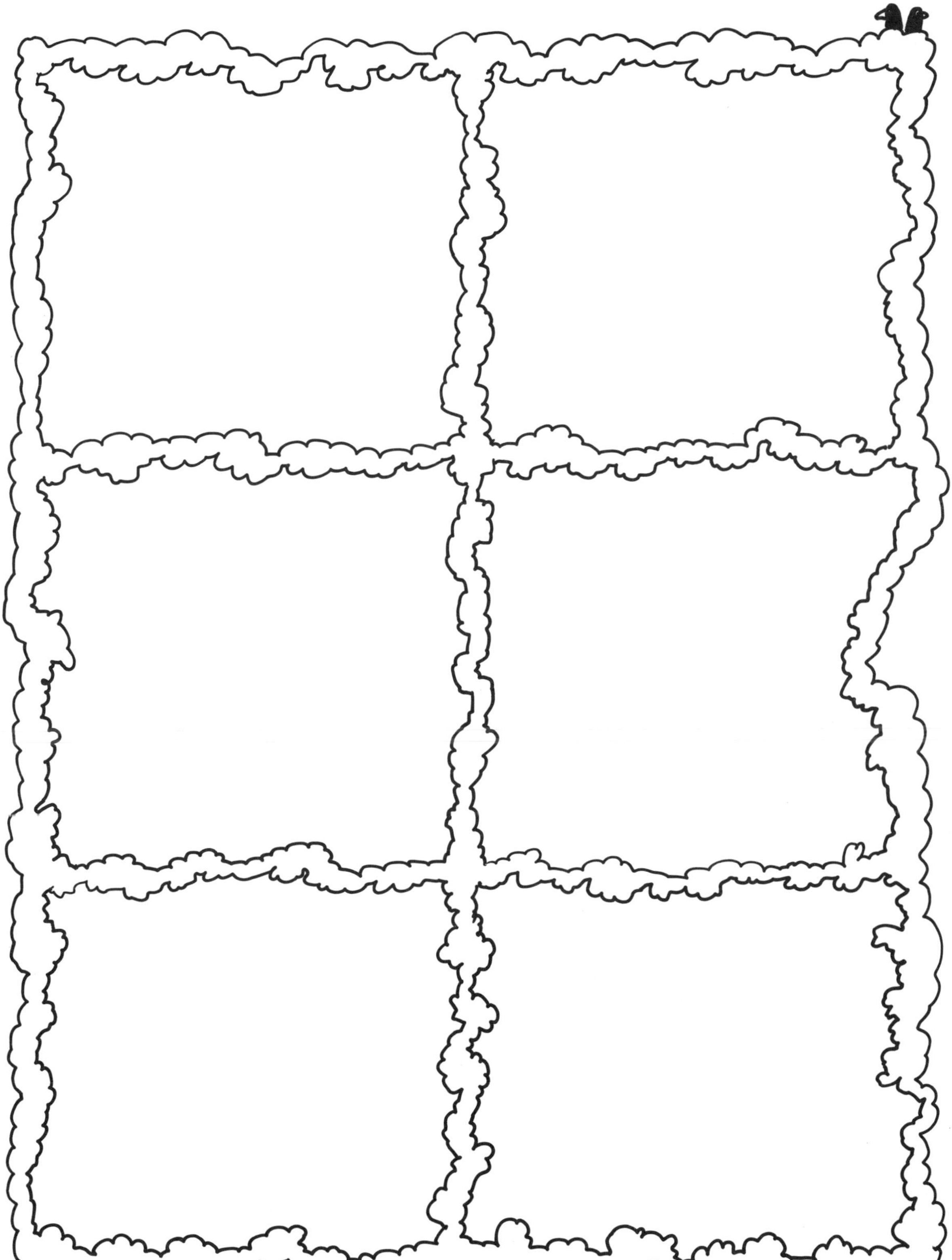

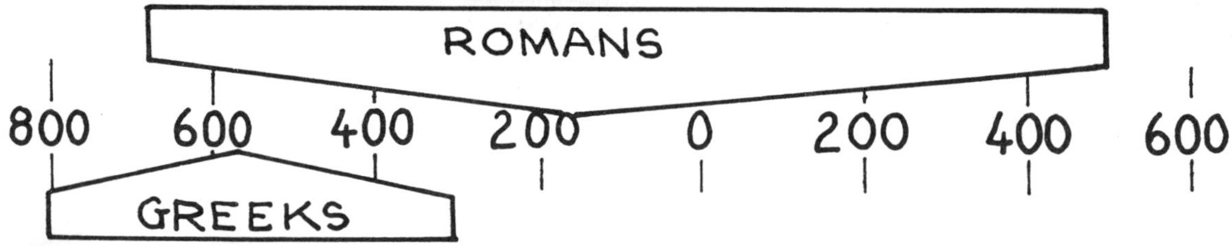

THE ELIZABETHANS

On an Elizabethan farm you may find these . . .
What do you think they are, and what are they used for?

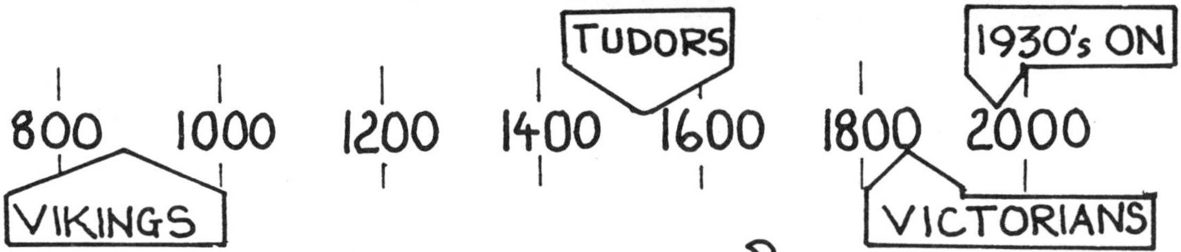

How do you think farms have changed from the Greek to the Elizabethan times? List some of the ways you think farms have changed.

____

____

Lots of sheep were kept in Elizabethan times. How different would the Elizabethan farmers' fields have been from the very small fields of the Viking farmers?

____

____

Even the common land – the land everyone could use to graze their animals – was taken over and used for sheep enclosures.

Why do you think sheep were important on Elizabethan farms?

____

____

____

____

Many new skills had to be learned by the farm workers. They had to learn all the processes involved in the production of the finished cloth that was made from the sheep's wool.

What are these people doing?

The sheep farmers became very rich, exporting their woollen cloth abroad.

The rich enjoyed good food. They ate breakfasts, dinners, and suppers. The big meal was dinner at about 12 o'clock which lasted a long time.
What do you eat at midday?

Elizabethans ate a lot of meat. Samuel Pepys, a diary writer of the times, described a meal . . .
'a brace of stewed carp, six roasted chickens, a jowl of salmon, a tanzy, two ox tongues and cheese!'
Pigeons stuffed with gooseberries, goose pie and buttered shrimps were popular too!

What do you think a tanzy was?

Draw an Elizabethan meal here . . . don't forget the vegetables!

Draw in the animals that were common on Elizabethan farms.

The Elizabethans enjoyed lots of different foods at their feasts.
Some they raised on their farms, some they hunted.
What food could have come from these hunts?

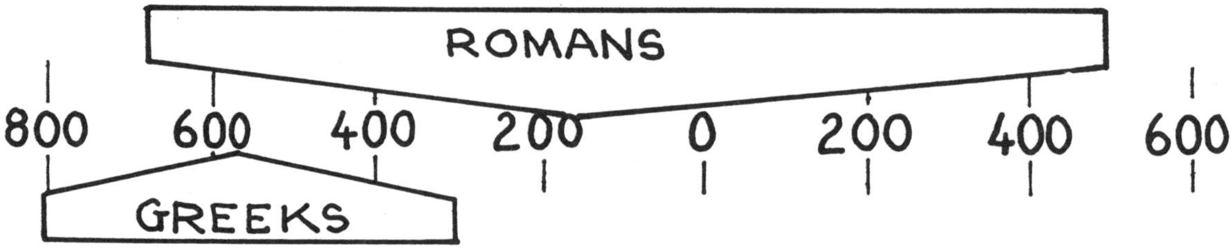

THE VICTORIANS

The people that worked on farms in Victorian times had very hard lives.

Houses were small, families were large! Water had to be collected from the pump or stand-pipe, and toilets were just an outside shed with a wooden seat over a cesspit.

Farm workers rose at about 5 a.m. to start work.

Breakfast was always the same – bread put into a bowl, sprinkled with salt and covered with hot water! This was known as kettlebroth and was washed down with a mug of sweet tea.

Lunch would be taken about 12 a.m. and bread and cheese were eaten.

The evening meal was the main meal of the day and would consist of a stew made from a piece of bacon or pork plus any vegetables available from the garden: potatoes, cabbage, turnip or onion. The bacon would be fatty and make the stew greasy!

A weekly shopping list would look like this . . .

bread	4s 8d
treacle	1d
sugar	9d
tea	6d
meat	2s 0d
cheese	4d

How does this differ from your weekly shopping? ______________________________

Make a list . . . with the prices! 5p is the equivalent of 1 s(hilling).

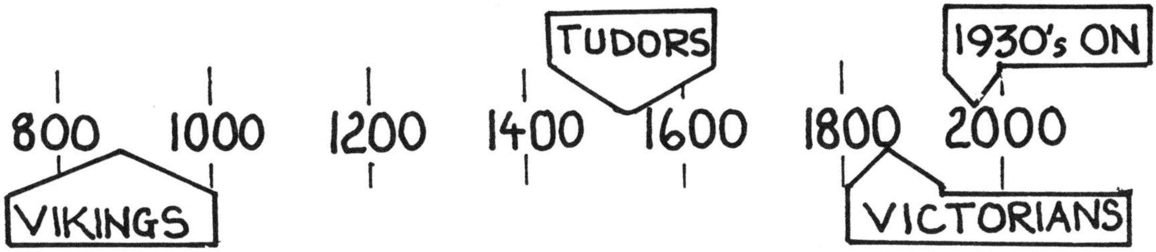

The pig was the saviour of the Victorian farmer. Most kept a pig and this was a real 'piggy bank'. It is said that the only bit of the pig that was wasted was its squeal.

Name all the different kinds of food that can be made from a pig!

Here is a Victorian Christmas Pudding.

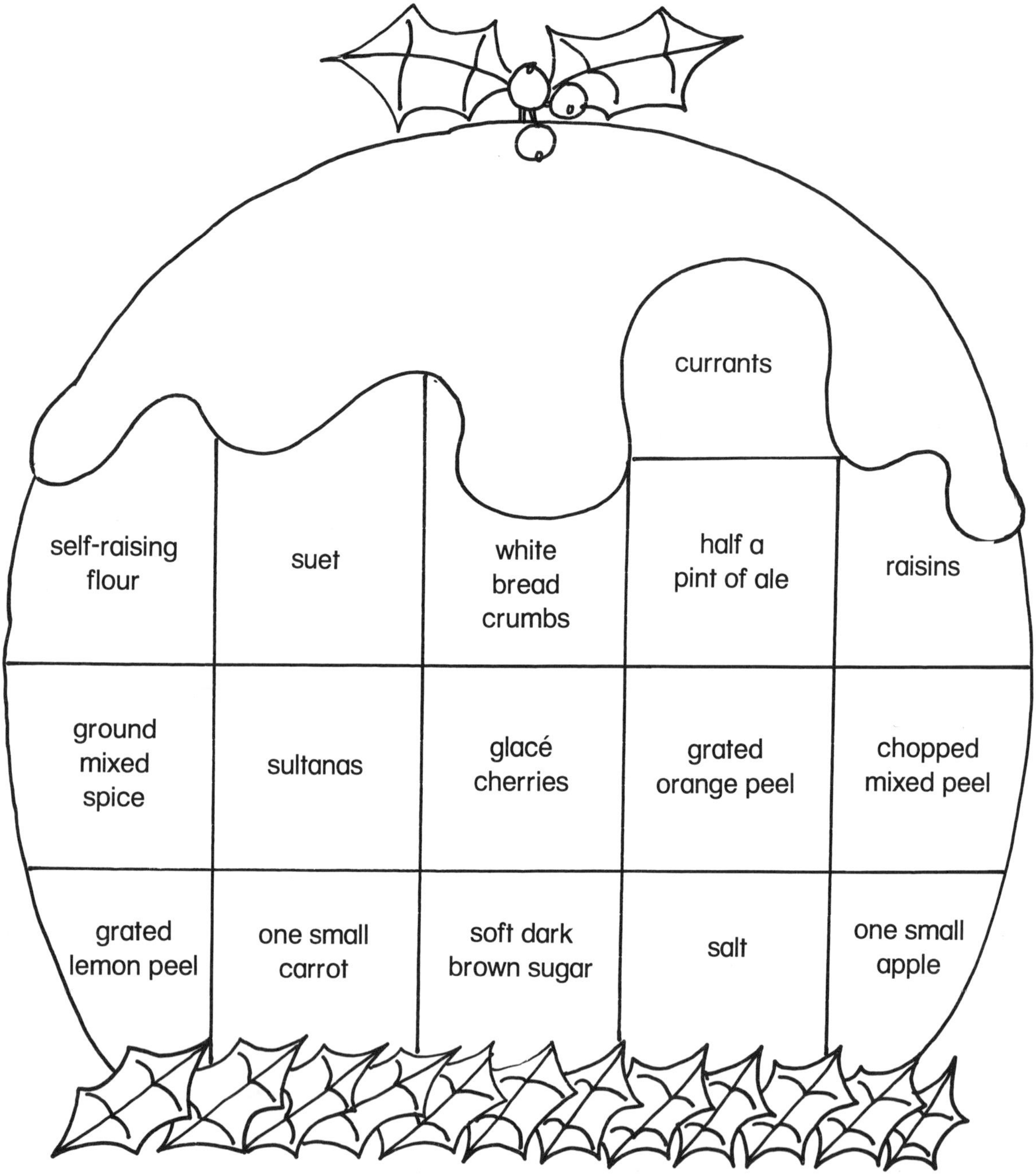

Draw or list all the things that had to be imported into England.

When a farm worker ploughed a field he walked about ten miles for each acre he ploughed! The Victorians were great inventors and many new machines began to appear on the farms.

What do you think these were for?

Here are some popular Victorian farm animals.
Divide up the animals into separate fields using only three straight fence sections.

At the end of the harvest, there were celebrations to give thanks for the past year's harvest and to wish for good harvests in the future.
Corn dollies were made with the last stalks of corn from the fields. The Church's celebration of harvest – the harvest festival – was reintroduced during Victorian times by the Reverend Robert Hawker, Vicar of Morwenstow, Devon.

This is the simplest corn dolly – The Bridget Cross.
Try and make one.

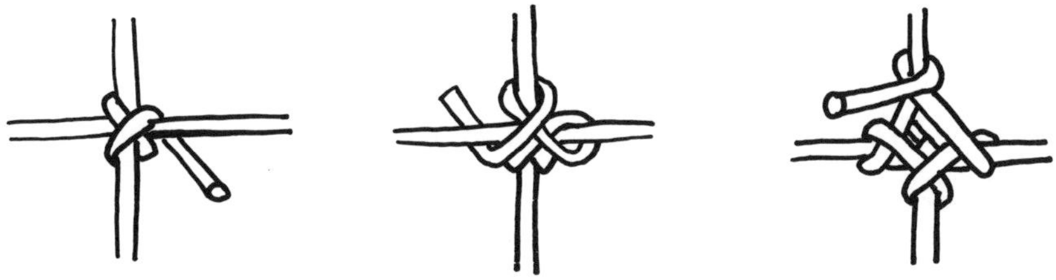

Keep weaving until you have finished the cross. If you have not got any straw, use drinking straws for your cross and weave with string.

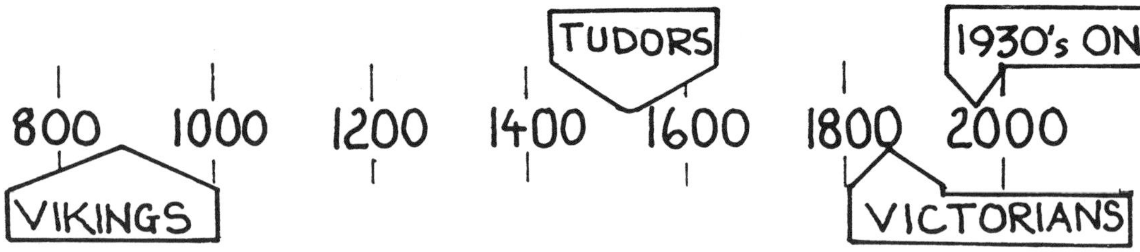

THE 1930s ONWARD

As people moved from the country into the towns, the farmers had to provide more food for people who were not producing food for themselves. Town houses were built very close together with little or no garden.

In 1939 when the Second World War broke out and food was difficult to import, home farming had to provide all necessary food. Sugar had always been cane sugar imported from the Caribbean and other hot places.

What crop was now grown for home produced sugar?

____

What other foods did people have to go without?

____

How were people stopped from buying as much food as they liked? ______________________________

With lots of men away at war, who do you think had to do the farm work? ______________________________

What was the name for this special group of people who worked the land? ______________________________

Pay for a minimum 50 hour week on the land was equivalent to £1.85 . . . a week!!!

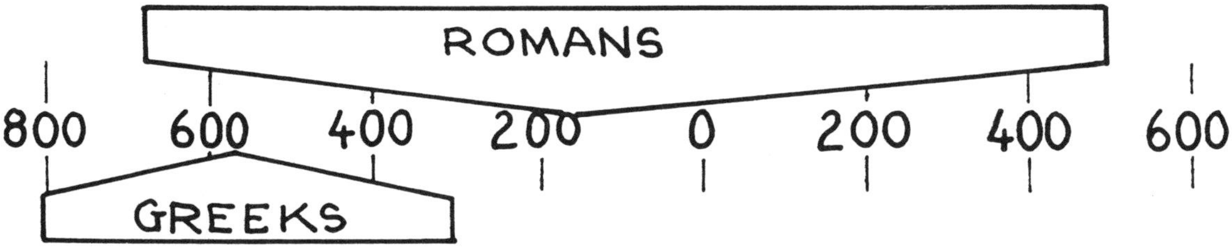

'Dig for Victory' were words that were used on posters during the war years.

What do you think the British people were being encouraged to do? Draw your poster here.

After the war, cities grew even larger.
Why do you think this happened? ______________________________

Even more food had to be grown on the farms to feed the people.

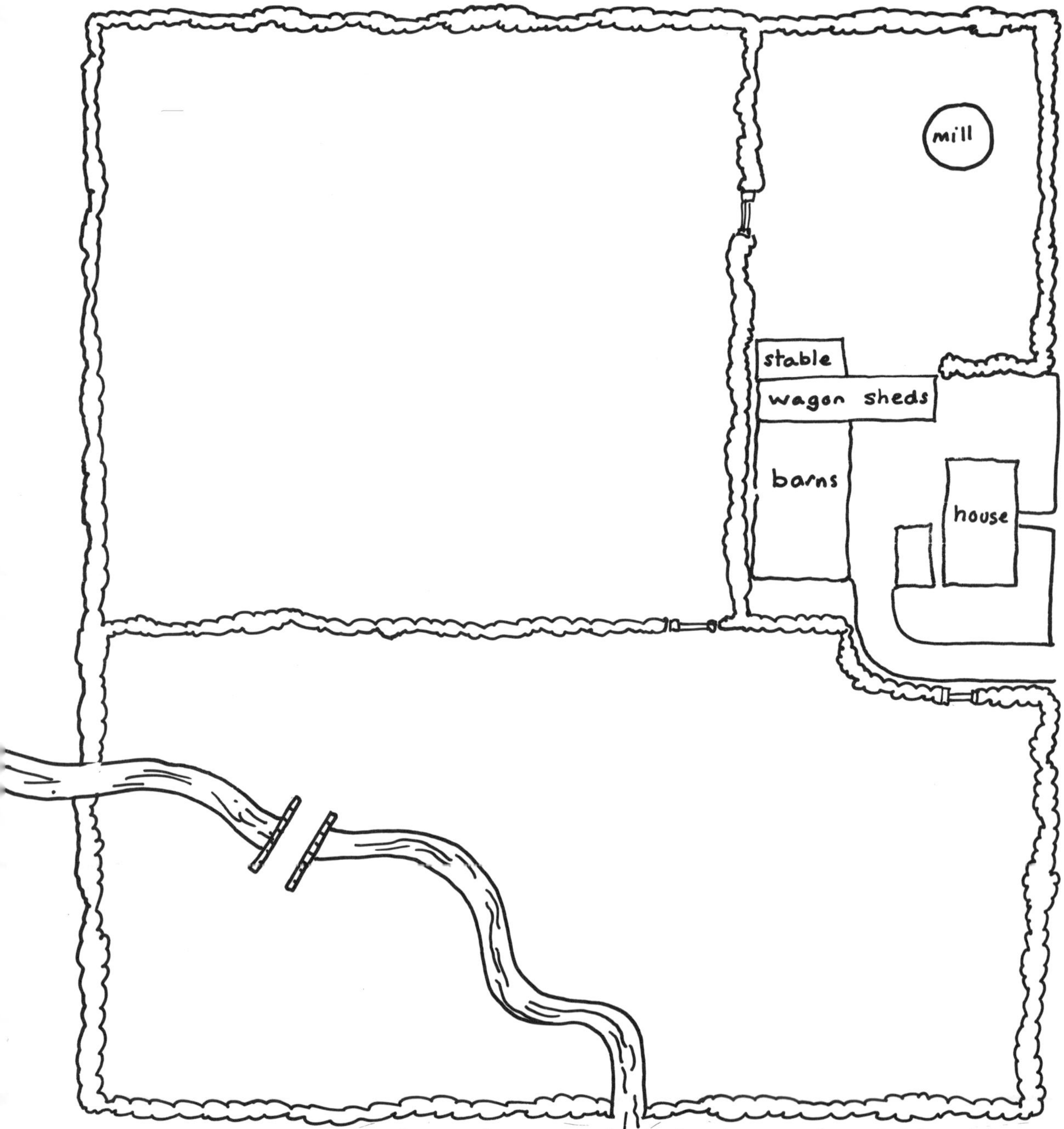

Here is the plan of a farm that was built in the early 1800s. How could it be changed into a dairy farm to provide milk for the new city trade?

These animals are found on British farms today.
What are they used for?

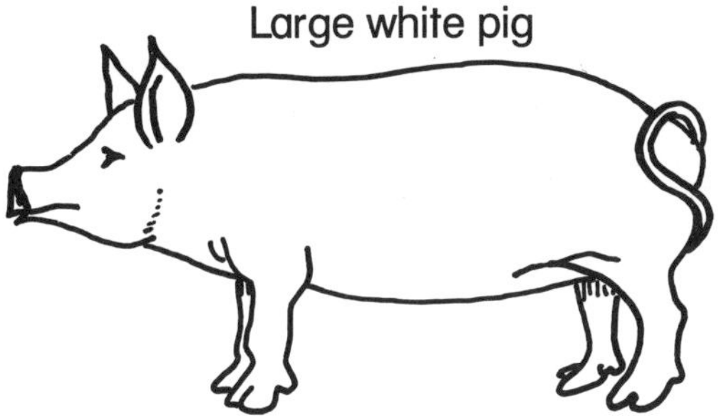
Large white pig

Suffolk sheep

British Friesian cow

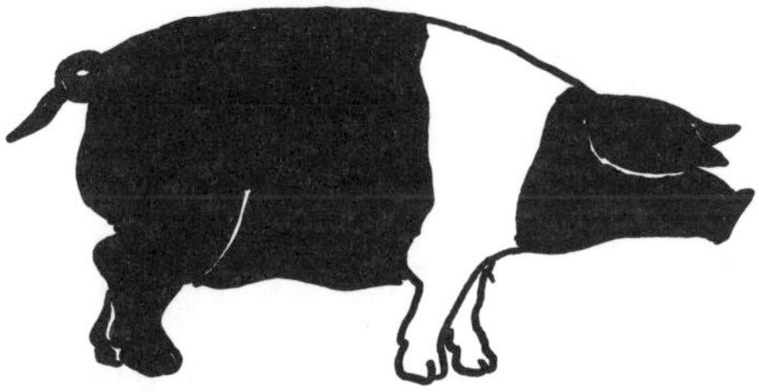
British saddleback pig

Border collie dog

Hereford bull

Look at the animals on the farms in the other parts of the book.
Which animals are no longer common on farms?

We are able to eat many different kinds of food because we can preserve food for storage. List some kinds of preserved food that you eat.

Now list some foods that the Greeks ate that had been preserved.

And some preserved Viking food.

And some preserved Elizabethan food.

And some preserved Victorian food.

Think of your favourite meal and draw or list it here.

Who might have shared your meal?

Food	Greeks	Vikings	Elizabethans	Victorians
beef				✓

Answers

p4 Cheese, figs, olives = lunch. Bread, wine = breakfast. Barley, porridge etc = dinner.
p5 Home: fish, wine, figs, barley, honey. Away: wheat, meat, spices.
p6 Goat, ox, sheep.
p7 Olives: oil. Grapes: wine.
p10 In the morning and in the evening. Salt came from salt pans on the coast.
p11 Different crops were grown in each strip each year.
p12 In the toilet pits!
p13 Cattle, chickens, goats, geese, pigs, sheep.
p14 Skip beehive: for keeping bees and getting honey. Post windmill: for grinding corn into flour. Plough: for digging the ground. Shepherd's hook or crook: for catching sheep. Drag: for preparing the ploughed field for sewing. Clippers: for shearing sheep.
p15 1. More machines, farms larger, farmers had lots of workers.
2. Fields would have to be well fenced.
3. Wool was very important for cloth. The Tudor farmers became very rich!
p16 Carding (straightening the wool fibres and cleaning out muck). Spinning the wool. Weaving the spun wool.
p17 A tanzy = a herb
p19 (clockwise) Deer and pheasant. Pigeons. Fish. Ducks.
p21 Sausages, haslet, black pudding, brawn, chitterlings, ham, trotters, etc.
p22 Currants, raisins, spice, sultanas, oranges, lemon and, in Victorian times, sugar.
p23 (clockwise) Cutting corn crops. Threshing. Ploughing.
A steam tractor for pulling the machines.
p26 Sugar beet.
Chocolate, bananas, oranges.
Rationing. The women.
The land army – made up of unmarried women.
p29 Large white pig: pork, bacon.
Suffolk sheep: mutton and wool.
British Friesian cow: milk, beef.
British saddleback pig: pork.
Border collie dog: rounds up sheep and cattle.
Hereford bull: beef.
p30 Greeks: raisins. Viking: salted pork.
Elizabethan: smoked eels. Victorian: candied peel.

p24

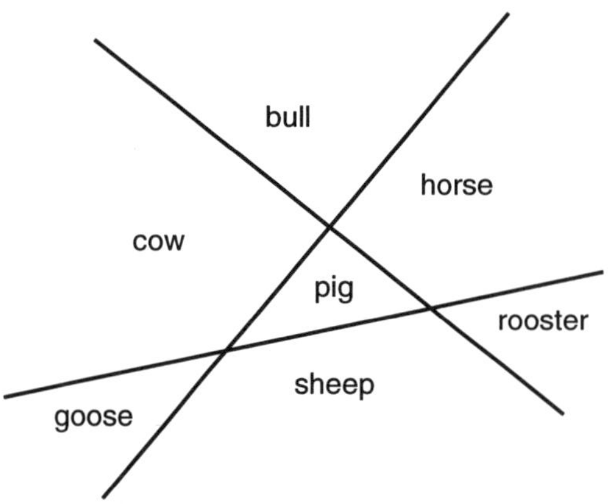

First published 1994 by Macmillan Children's Books, a division of Macmillan General Books Ltd
Cavaye Place London SW10 9PG and Basingstoke
Associated companies throughout the world

ISBN 0 330 33390 9

9 8 7 6 5 4 3 2 1

A CIP catalogue record for this book is available from the British Library.

Printed and bound in Great Britain by Henry Ling Ltd, The Dorset Press, Dorchester